How to Get Hired

Practical tips for successful employment

Ahmadreza Nakhjavani

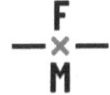

©Firouz Media 2022
All rights reserved

All rights reserved by the publisher. No parts of this publication may be reproduced, stored in a retrieval system, or transmitted in any form or by any means, electronic, mechanical, photocopying, recording, or otherwise, without the prior permission of the publisher.

ISBN: 978-1-7396603-7-6

Firouz Media
www.firouzmedia.com
contact@firouzmedia.com
IG: @firouzmedia

Author:
Ahmadreza Nakhjavani

Dedicated to those who have sat still and have been waiting for a miracle to be hired under the pretext of destiny.

Preface

Working in large enterprises for three decades has given me the opportunity to lecture in tens of seminars and student gatherings in universities sharing my experience mostly with youth.

Among the different topics of my lectures, nothing has been as interesting as the subjects related to recruitment and employment in companies and organizations.

As far as I do not believe in miracle or shortcut, I have done my best to show the audience how to succeed in recruiting with less mistakes by means of planning and endeavour.

As I have interviewed hundreds of employment applicants over the years, I have observed many frequent and common mistakes which can be simply rectified. Therefore, I decided to write this book. In fact, the main aim of this book is to share practical tips and guidelines to improve the quality of job interviews and increase the chance of applicants' recruitment.

In the first chapter of the book, I have reviewed some basic and important assumptions for recruitment in companies and organizations.

In the second chapter, I have explained how to choose the desired place to work, as many of applicants apply for employment without any future plans or knowing what they really need. This is the main reason behind many position and job movements only a few months after getting hired.

In the third chapter, the main attractions and comparative advantages of applicants are explained from the viewpoint of employers.

The fourth chapter illustrates the main tips on attending recruitment interviews. These tips will increase the quality of how we present ourselves in job interviews and the chance of being recruited.

While, in the final chapter, I have assumed that you are hired in a company and tried to discuss how to accelerate your success and growth procedures.

I hope this book will be fruitful for those who read it.

Ahmadreza Nakhjavani
    Tehran, 2022

How to Get Hired
Practical tips for successful employment

Ahmadreza Nakhjavani

Chapter one:
Basic pre-employment assumptions

Please read the following sentences once and evaluate them in your mind:

- Unemployment of educated people is high in this country.
- To find a job, you must always be on the lookout for opportunities and have luck.
- To enter the job market, you need the help of a nepotist.
- Successful people in organizations are connected to people in higher positions.

If you believe these statements, I must honestly declare that you have wasted your money on buying this book. I recommend that you, at least, do not waste your time reading it, because this book cannot be effective for someone with such attitude or mindset.

In fact, none of the aforementioned statements are true if you are looking for a job in the private sector or one where you are going to be paid by means of your own hard work. I have no opinion about the organizations that receive funding from the government, and for many of these organizations,

the criteria for employment are different and outside the scope of my recommendations.

Although the statistics of developing countries show that their unemployment rates are relatively high, I believe that what respected unemployed people suffer from is lack of skills and knowledge. In reality, I reckon that we do not have skilled and knowledgeable unemployed people in most of countries.

What such countries suffer from is that there is a large group of educated young people who fail to find work, but when you talk to them, you find that regardless of their degree, they have kept very limited material in their minds from years of study. I have experienced the bitter truth in interview sessions where a job applicant is unable to talk for ten minutes about their field of study; what was studied at university for four to seven years. Surprisingly, an immediate response to this question, "What did you learn at university?" is "They do not teach anything in universities!"

Although I do not deny the weaknesses of education systems in many countries, I believe that if the students learn the taught university courses, they will not be unemployed even if they study in the rarest or least used academic fields.

Likewise, I have the same opinion about general skills. If we consider working with computer and typing skills and using basic software (such as Word and Excel) as basic skills, having these skills guarantees that the job seeker will not be unemployed. Fluency in English, in addition to these skills, can completely change and improve one's prospects. Now, imagine how the situation would change if the job seeker had specialized skills in addition to these general ones.

I have repeatedly witnessed this unpleasant experience when a friend or acquaintance, out of pity, have introduced me to someone who is unemployed and surprisingly said that the person has a master's degree in a field. After interviewing these individuals, I have never found out that, contrary to popular beliefs, he or she learned something at university or at least has basic skills.

Last year, I travelled to a province to finalize a contract with one of the largest organizations in the country. When I noticed an unusual delay in starting the meeting, I was told that the computer in the meeting was unlabelled with Persian alphabets on the keyboard and none of the ten managers and experts present at the meeting could type with it. I was surprised and asked to sit at the computer, they could not believe that a manager of a big organization was able to type without looking at the keyboard!

I hope you now realize how easy it is to be different in organizations and what skills can help you to be hunted and hired in organizations.

I have mentioned "chance." If we hope for chance, endeavour is no longer meaningful. If you do not hope for chance, destiny or unseen forces, you know you must rely on yourself and your efforts.

If you listen to industry and organization managers and ask them about their problems, in their very first words, you will hear about the lack of suitable or specialized manpower. That's why I advise my young friends; if you have something to offer, do not wait for the publication of employment advertisements of organizations. Arbitrarily submit your application and resume to organizations that are suitable for the employment you want.

One of the problems we have with some of our friends applying for jobs is their over confidence and unrealistic image of themselves.

Let me give you a simple example. When asked about their mastery of the general software (already mentioned), almost every one of them claim to work masterfully with it. However, as soon as the first question is asked, you hear, "I have to check it at my computer." Or when you ask about the meaning of a few simple English words, you sometimes hear, "I've been away for a while." I am not saying that these people are making false claims, but I've found that some of them do not have a true and realistic image of themselves. This is ironically better that in order to grow more, one must be strict about themselves and challenge themselves more hostilely in their personal comfort zone.

With this relatively long introduction, I would like to draw your attention to some very basic advice on employment assumptions.

1. Having a specific future plan in work and life

My initial assumption for jobseekers to be present at the interview is that they know why they are sitting in the job interview and have a specific plan for their future. Therefore, the job interview is precisely in line with the goal(s) they have set for their future.

The character in "Alice in Wonderland" (by Lewis Carroll) encounters a cat at a crossroads, and when she asks the cat which path to choose, the cat in return asks Alice where she would go and she replies, "I do not know." The cat then answers, "When you do not know where you want to go, go any way you want."

This is the story of some job seekers who submit resumes for all the jobs that are announced so that eventually one of their tries will work.

This poses another risk, while reducing the likelihood of being hired, especially for professional interviewers. In fact, those who take a job unplanned or perfunctorily are far more likely to be dissatisfied and change jobs. If I want to be the sales and marketing manager of a reputable and successful organization in the next five years, then today I should be looking for jobs that are in line with this goal, rather than sending out resumes to just about any organization that is hiring for unrelated jobs and hoping for luck.

For this, you need to have an "individual or personal development plan" or so-called "IDP" or "PDP." Although we are not naturally organized individuals, having a plan is unavoidable and I recommend that you write your plans down. To do this, simply search the Internet for the words IDP or PDP to find thousands of scientific or social media sites that generously provide free templates of this plan. The main basis or framework of a personal development plan is for you to gauge where you are now with the knowledge, skills, and competencies you have and assess where you want to go in the next few years understanding what skills, knowledge, and competencies you need to reach that goal.

My emphasis on the topic of a personal development plan is that sometimes not attending a job interview session that has nothing to do with our future goal and avoiding its aftermath is far better than attending and being hired.

2. Having basic general skills

In my view, in the current recruitment market of many countries, manpower suffers from the lack of general and basic skills that job seekers, by mastering these skills, can easily get hired. Let me claim that if a person is only fluent in their country's formal language and English typing, he or she will not be unemployed, let alone spice up these general skills with other skills. The most important general skills you need to learn are:

A) Fluency in formal language

It may be strange to say that many of us are not fluent in the formal language of our country. We cannot write a letter or a text correctly, and similarly, we have serious weaknesses in expressing content, formal presentations, and speeches. While mastering formal language is one of the skills that is required for all jobs.

B) Country's formal language and English typing

I think there is no need to explain that typing is the basic necessity of working in most organizations. To get an idea of how well you know this, there are several websites available on the Internet where you can measure your typing skills.

C) Mastery of general application software

Ability to work with operating systems (such as

Windows) and software pieces such as Word, Excel and PowerPoint are a must. Initial acquaintance is not enough and they should be well mastered by job seekers.

Fortunately, there are so many free books and content on the Internet that you can master the software on your own. To fix a problem, the answer to all the problems can be found on the Internet as well.

D) Relative proficiency in English

In a world where the borders of countries are becoming virtual and our connection with the world is getting closer, the need to master English increases. What is more, in many corporate jobs, knowing English is a competitive advantage over other job seekers. At the same time, knowing English is undeniably important if you want to use online resources for learning.

***

If we consider the contents of this chapter as the initial assumptions for being hired, we can plan to attend an interview session. If you feel unqualified when it comes to these prerequisites, you need to take immediate action to address them.

Chapter two:
How to choose the right organization?

It is enough for the jobseeker to taste unemployment for a while or to have a lot of economic pressure to run the risk of sending resume to all the organizations that have job openings.

I've seen a lot of friends who send their resumes wherever they can, and in many cases, it does not matter where the organization they may be hired is located or what the future holds. They even send resumes to different jobs, like someone who throws their boat into the water and leave the choice of destination to the fate of the wind!

With this introduction, it is very important to choose the organization in which we are going to be hired. After all, how many times in our lives do we have the opportunity to choose a workplace?

In my view, choosing a place to work is very similar to getting married, where both parties must choose the right one. Unfortunately, some job seekers are only concerned with whether or not the organization chooses them; they do not have a specific precondition or plan.

To choose the right organization, and assuming that we have a specific goal for the future according to what has been said in the previous pages, we must ask ourselves what we will achieve by being employed in the organization that intends to hire us. Basically, our most important achievements from being hired in an organization are:

1. Salary and benefits
2. Education and learning
3. Social status
4. Job security and reliability
5. Work environment

After telling this, let's continue the argument with an anecdote. Once upon a time, a baby camel asked its mother, "Why are our soles wide?"

And the mother replied, "When we walk in the desert, our feet will not sink in the sand."

The baby camel then asked, "Why are our lips so thick?" And the mother answered,

"So that we can pull the thorns out of the ground with our lips."

And the baby camel asked again, "What is this bulge on our back?"

"It is called hump, and is the best food store for us who have to endure thirst in the desert," said the mother.

The baby camel finally asked, "So what are we doing at the zoo?"

This is the story of some of us who, with all the specific plans we have, we get hired in organizations where we have to immediately ask ourselves, "What am I doing here?"

In fact, salary and compensation are our first goal in the organization where we are going to be hired. Obviously, it plays a very key role in choosing an organization, but that does not mean that we can ignore other goals.

Many years have passed since we were first hired by an organization and we may be faced with this question: What have we achieved through these years spent in the organization? That is why my advice to all young audiences of this book is that if you are constantly doing repetitive work in the organization and your skills or knowledge are not being developed, be concerned. In addition, those who seek to grow in organizations or seek personal development should expose themselves to learning or challenging their knowledge and skills in the organization.

With that being said, the jobs in organizations that bring us learning and training have hidden benefits, and this should not be overlooked.

Part of our nature is satisfied by the formation of the social status and brand position resulting from our job. For this reason, it is very different whether we work in a well-known company or somewhere anonymous. Working in anonymous companies is not a problem, especially since we have to look at the set of achievements mentioned, we may be working in a place where the salary alone is worth not gaining other achievements. In any case, the benefits of working in well-known companies cannot be denied.

Job reliability and security is another achievement that may not be found in some jobs. In particular, we should be comfortable working in an organization where we can count on salaries every month, while not having to worry that the owners of the organization may flee the country unexpectedly and as we enter the workplace, a group of creditors will gather in front of the organization making demands.

Finally, we spend most of our lives in the organization, rather than at home. Therefore, the extent at which we enjoy these moments in life is very important, as much as who we share them with and how much energy we get from them. For example, there may be some organizations in some countries where the workforce may have to pretend to have a particular worldview or mindset. Unfortunately, there are many organizations that often refine the beliefs and inner attitudes of job seekers in order to hire them, and the force that accepts to work in such organizations must always be careful in its behaviour as the organization requires.

Considering these goals/requirements, no one but the job applicant himself can say in general to what extent these achievements of the organization are in line with his needs and wants. To do this, we need to research to find out which of our needs will be met by the organization that publishes the job advertisement.

* * *

With this hasty explanation, the author assumes that the job seeker who has a clear plan for his future does enough research about the organization and does not forget that the only achievement of working with an organization is not a salary, and evaluates cooperation with the organization from different aspects.

Chapter three:
Attractions of the job applicant

A job interview is a space where we present our capabilities to the organization, so how we present our strengths is very important. At the same time, it is necessary to point out that nothing but reality is to be discussed in the meeting.

Perhaps it would be better to elaborate the issue in this way that even if the most professional, pretentious people exaggerate their capabilities, it will be clear in a matter of a few months what they really are capable of, and ironically, they will pay more as a result.

In fact, it is about behaving well when we present all our abilities and capabilities in short interviews so that we will be hired.

Consequently, we need to keep in mind what is interesting to the interviewer. Obviously, a set of issues can be interesting for the interviewer which are so lengthy that I will only elaborate the main ones.

1. Passion and energy for work

What top managers of the organizations are suffering from today is the lack of enthusiasm and energy among the youth, compared to the past. Accordingly, from the interviewer's point of view, there is nothing more interesting than energy and enthusiasm.

It's your art to have both the desire to build in your heart and to show it in an interview. For example, if I feel in an interview that the applicant has the basics, I give them homework to do and measure their enthusiasm. For instance, I give them a book and I want them to read the book in the next few days and write their opinion for me, whether in several lines or several pages. I do not set a specific time and I leave it all up to the applicant to see how eager they are to do so.

If the applicant really has the enthusiasm and energy to be hired—and if I were them—They would not sleep at night to read the book sooner

and submit their opinion. The painful point is that, according to experience, few applicants will read the book, and there have even been cases where I have asked the applicant to do so, and the applicant has proudly stated that they have no interest or time to do so. Now, the question is this: If a job seeker who desires to be hired by a well-known company of the country (and even let's say an anonymous company) is not willing to read the book we gift them, are they qualified to be hired?
I even recommend that you yourself as the applicant offer to be given homework. This action has a great impact on conveying a sense of passion.

2. Having a clear plan for the future

When I ask about the applicant's five-year plan in interview sessions, I sometimes find that it is as if the interviewee is facing this question for the first time in his or her life. Another major group provides general answers, like: "I want to be successful and have a good job."
Now, suppose the applicant says, "I will have finished improving upon my general skills, such as English, in the next five years ... I will be defending

my doctoral dissertation, and I will be working for a large organization as a Marketing Manager. In my personal life, after defending my dissertation, I will get married." How will you feel as an interviewer?

Because I have talked about the importance of personal planning in previous chapters, I do not see the need for further writing and I have promised myself that I will convey the content in such a way that the book will not get lengthy and boring. For this reason, I would only like to point out that having a clear plan for the future demonstrates to the interviewer that the job seekers is looking for both growth and dynamism to achieve a specific goal and career path. Therefore, they will not change their future path due to excitement or cross-cutting offers, and there is nothing more ideal for the organization.

3. Having presentable achievements in life and work

It is more in movies and legends that one person suddenly changes into a new one, and if a change is to take place, it is a long-term process with specific difficulty and planning. In this way, people's pasts largely predict their future, and the interviewer, looking at their record in life and work, can principally predict the path to future growth.

How can a person who has not had any tangible and presentable achievements (even in personal life) over decades of their life, change in a short period of time and bring remarkable achievement(s) to our organization?

From the interviewer's point of view, even if the job applicant has achieved something in their personal life (e.g. they have won a medal or a position in sports competitions, even in the education district of their city, or have learned to play a musical instrument), it can be a sign that they have a habit or history of trying to achieve a goal or not.

Therefore, having achievements in life or work is something that attracts organizations, and if you have such achievements, you should definitely mention them in an interview session anyway.

If you have nothing to offer, you have to ask yourself; how many more years do I have to build on such achievements?

4. Relative stability in past jobs

As mentioned earlier, the relative stability of the applicant's past jobs gives the organization a sense of confidence that the applicant has a long-term vision for the future or that it will proceed according to a specific plan. Applicants who have worked in a different organization (and even worse, in a variety of jobs) raise the question in the mind of the interviewer as to how challenging the applicants have been to previous employers or at best, suggests that the applicant is a confused and unplanned person.

Now that we want to attend an interview session, this is not something that we can think of, but in any case, it is good to always have it in mind and be aware of the consequences.

5. Being different from other applicants

In most cases, interview sessions are held when the

organization has advertised for employment and a group of applicants attends the sessions one after the other.

In this case, you should be present at the interview in a way that sets you apart from other job seekers in any way. This distinction can be both in your experience and skills, and background and knowledge, and can be demonstrated to the interviewer in the management of the interview session (such as the demonstration of passion and energy).

What you will read on the next pages are an attempt to show this distinction.

Chapter four:
Important tips for a job interview session

As a reader of this book, you may have wanted to have these employment recommendations sooner, but so far, it was necessary to emphasize the necessity of having a specific plan and goal, choosing an organization, and so on before. There are still other things to do before attending a job interview.

In other words, pre-session preparation is no less important, if not more important than the interview session itself. This is similar to negotiation principles[1], which always emphasize that the negotiator must act in a Pareto principle and devote eighty percent of his energy to pre-meeting preparation.

---

[1] Wilfredo Federico Damaso Pareto is an Italian sociologist and economist (1848-1923) whose 80/20 rule is well known in the science of management.

In general, you need to take steps before the interview session to be fully prepared to attend the job interview. Here are some important steps:

Job interview pre-attending Tips

1. Prepare a good and simple resume

Perhaps it is strange that one of the biggest weaknesses of job seekers is the lack of a principled and, at the same time, simple resume.

A good resume should not be too concise or too detailed. The content should be arranged in such a way that the most important strengths and answers to the main questions of the interviewer are identified at a glance. In the following lines, the most important questions are reflected, which can also be used in writing a resume. However, ready-made resume templates are readily available on several websites.

2. Gain complete knowledge of the organization

Although I have already highlighted the

importance of choosing an appropriate organization, it is significant to become fully acquainted with the organization before attending the interview. It's unbelievable to me that I see so many job seekers who come for interviews but have not once bothered to read the organization's website!

The easiest way to get acquainted with an organization is to read the organization's website word by word and then search the internet. It would be great if you could attend the interview session with information about the following:

- General information about the organization (number of employees, general history, and so on.)
- The most important areas of activity
- Market position and share (and names of competitors)
- The most important features or advantages of products and services

Knowing this information has nothing to do with the job for which you may be hired, and having this information is essential for any activity you are going to engage in and can be useful in an interview session.

3. Getting information about the interviewer

Knowing the interviewer can greatly help you in your interview session. It can at least alleviate your anxiety during the interview. Also, in an interview session, you may be able to gently (and so-called subcutaneously) remind the interviewer that you know them somehow and convey the sense that being hired in the organization is crucial to the interviewer.

In addition, remember that it is not strange at all to ask, "Who will I have the honour of being interviewed by?" when they call you to schedule an interview session. Then you can search the internet and social media in order to know the person and their character.

4. Researching and getting acquainted with the job description offered

As mentioned earlier, it is assumed that the job applicant is choosing the job in accordance with the applicant's own specific plan. For this purpose, you can write down all the questions you have about the job position to ask in the interview session. However, I recommend that you read about the job offered and search the internet. There are various scientific databases that help a lot[2].

As you become more familiar with the job description, not only can you attend the interview session with more fluency and confidence, and in the interview session, show the interviewer that you are well aware of its organizational position, it will also help you ask any questions you may have about this job. In addition, no one can find the commonalities of the job and your skills and knowledge, and possibly present them in the meeting better than you.

---

[2] You can search for the job title in search engines like Google along with words like Job Description. You can even add the industry name in which you might be hired. For example, the advertisement states that a cement company is looking for a product manager. You can search for: job description of product manager in cement.
As an example, I recommend visiting this organization's website: www.onetonline.org

For example, suppose you are going to be hired by a foreign trading company and you are an IT expert in terms of knowledge and skills. In an interview meeting, you can speak like:

- In a foreign trading company, correspondence and documentation are very important and I can implement office automation in your company.
- The unavailability of the corporate network can cause significant damage to the company and I can stabilize the corporate internal network in such a way that its availability is never less than 99.9 percent.
- With the help of IT tools, I can create a dashboard that is aware of Operation Level Agreement (OLA) and increases the agility of the organization.

These were basic examples. I recommend writing down your tips and consulting with experts in the field in which you work.

5. Practice answering common questions

One of the most important tips I can give you is to practice answering common interview questions. The mystery remains unanswered for me, as I have interviewed many job seekers who are stunned when asked a simple question (such as "speak about your knowledge and skills") as if it is the first time they are hearing this question in their lives and they have never asked it to themselves either. I then find myself having to explain in detail what I mean when I talk about knowledge and skills!

Basically, the most important interview questions you need to be prepared to answer are less than ten questions. Therefore, it is imperative to prepare an answer to these questions.

The most important questions that you may be asked and need to be answered enthusiastically are:

- Tell us about yourself[3].

---

[3] You should briefly and efficiently state the most important qualities you have. You need to say how old you are, what your education is, what your most important knowledge and expertise are, and where you want to go in your career.

How to Get Hired

- Talk about your skills and knowledge[4].
- What are the most important outputs you have at work?[5]
- What's your strength points?[6]
- What's your weakness?[7]
- Why did you leave your pervious job?[8]

---

[4] Avoid general statements and specifically talk about your skills and knowledge. For example: In the field of sales and marketing, I am good at preparing a marketing plan, and in the field of digital marketing, I have implemented SEO and SEM strategies.

[5] Many of us choose general and cliché answers for this question. For example, "I have good public relations," or "I get everything done on time," while these are not clear outputs.

[6] In this regard, you can point out your moral qualities or experiences that can be positive or even help you in work and life. For example: "As I started with face-to-face marketing, I found myself good at sales negotiations and I developing a better understand of customer rights."

[7] One of the ironic points of interview sessions is that many of us redefine our strengths when expressing our weaknesses. For example, some will say: "I am too kind" or "I do not think about my health because of too much responsibility!" While we must speak honestly about this, we must relate it to the role we are being interviewed for. For example: "The world of marketing in the world has changed and my knowledge in this area needs to be improved and modified."

[8] There is nothing better than honesty in answering an interview question. Even if you left an organization because of a mistake or misuse, declare it. Admitting mistakes is sometimes a symbol of your power and strong personality. Never seek justification. The interviewer can see how honestly you are speaking by a little intelligence and looking at your body language.

- How can you help our organization?[9]
- What are some of the biggest past achievements you've had?[10]
- What are your long-term goals?[11]

The more time you spend answering these questions, the more your chances of success are in an interview.

6. Eat before the interview session

This advice may sound strange, but proper nutrition before the interview session is important. If you attend the meeting thirsty and hungry, it is very likely that you will not have the energy to do the interview and even your mind will not help you to answer the questions you are asked. You may have the experience of sitting in long university exams, when your energy depletes so that even when you know the answers to the questions, you

---

[9] This was discussed in the previous lines.

[10] This was discussed in the previous lines.

[11] In the first chapter, this was discussed in detail.

feel exhausted and want to deliver the exam sheet as soon as possible. Hence, it is a good idea to pay attention to your diet before the interview and even have some chocolate or anything that raises your blood sugar in your bag.

7. Choose the right attire to attend the meeting

Proper clothing is very important in the interview session. The dress you will wear in the interview session should be formal and, most importantly, ordinary and in accordance with the custom of the community.

A survey of 2,000 interviewers found that 70 percent of interviewers were not interested in overly fashionable applicants. The results also show that, if they are faced with deciding between two applicants, 65% of them declared that the applicants' clothing will play a key role in making their decision.

***

Tips for an interview session

If you follow these tips before attending the interview, I can draw your attention to some of the recommendations during the interview:

1. Attending an interview earlier

If you arrive late for an interview for any reason, the first negative thing about you will form in the interviewer's mind, and even if the interviewer is a little strict like the writer, he or she may avoid doing the interview. Believe me, excuses like car crashes and crowded streets are no longer as effective as they used to be. Even if the interviewer ignores the delay, you will get anxious and the effects will be evident in the quality of your responses in the meeting.

Accordingly, plan so that you have enough time to arrive at the meeting (taking into account unforeseen events). Moreover, your earlier presence may give you the opportunity to gain more information by walking around the building, or to become calm if, for whatever reason, you are tense and nervous.

2. Do not underestimate yourself

Although I talked about your inner anxiety in the meeting, I only talked about it based on experience. After all, why bother with a simple dialogue session? In other words, despite all the points that have been mentioned so far, sitting in an interviewer's chair does not mean that he or she is superior to you in terms of knowledge and experience. Moreover, in my opinion, the job seeker should be skilled and educated enough to attend the meeting with full confidence and know that now it is the organization that wants to make every effort to hire him. So, my advice is not to underestimate yourself in any way and do not lose confidence owing to the aristocratic atmosphere of the organization or the superior attitude of the interviewer. Do not forget that the interview is a meeting where both parties want to see if they have anything in common. Therefore, the two sides are supposed to choose each other. Hence, do not underestimate yourself.

3. We must know the etiquette well

One of the obvious weaknesses of some of us is the lack of familiarity in observing social etiquette. In this regard, Persian sources are very limited and incomplete. On the other hand, non-Persian sources are written based on Western culture.

All in all, there are many things we need to learn and apply in an interview (and in life in general). Let me mention just a few simple examples and leave the further reading to the reader:

- The interviewee should not reach out and shake hands until the interviewer reaches out.
- We need to stand beside the table until the interviewer asks us to sit.
- We should not put our overcoat (or coat) on the back of a chair, and if we have to take it off for any reason, we should get permission and hang it on a hanger.
- Do not put cubic sugar or chocolate in the corner of your mouth to drink tea. We have to dissolve it in the cup and if a spoon is not available, drink the tea without sugar.

- It is better to be a little patient so that the tea or coffee cools down so that we do not have to drink it in such a way that we can hear the sound of liquids sipping.
- At the end of the session, say something like, "Am I allowed to leave?"
- At the end of the session, place the chair behind the desk and, if the interview is conducted on a glass desk, wipe with a tissue to remove your fingerprints.

4. Take notes

One of the basic requirements of any meeting is to have a notebook and a pen to write the important points of the meeting. I do not remember meeting with professional friends and seeing someone in the meeting without a notebook and a pen. The Chinese have a proverb that says, "The lightest ink is better than the strongest memory."

Job interview sessions are not out of the ordinary and you need to have a notebook and a pen with you. By taking notes, you are first and foremost sending the message to the interviewer how accurate and adherent you are to the rules. On the other hand, by writing the questions, you can be sure that no point is missed. During the conversation, if you come up with a sudden remark, you can write it down.

5. Answer the questions specifically

One of the issues that can confuse the interviewer in the meeting is avoiding answering questions or speaking vaguely and indirectly in general. It often happens to me that I ask a simple question and I expect the interviewee to answer directly and without zooming out or in, but mostly I have to point out, "You have not answered my question yet." It is interesting that sometimes these warnings will not work.

Be careful that you answer the questions directly and without zooming out, and even if you need to give an explanation that is out of the direct answer, admit it yourself. For example: "I have not answered your questions yet, but let me point out that…"

Do not forget that the interviewer's patience and attention to hearing your content is limited, and therefore, you should ultimately answer simply and concisely, and if necessary, declare you are ready to go into more detail. Even saying things like, "Was my answer enough for this question?" or "Did you get the answer to your question?" works very well.

6. You manage the meeting

I do not remember where I read this English anecdote: "The lab rat told his friend; I have conditioned this scientist. He gives me a piece of cheese every time I shake my hand!"
Like the hidden irony of this story that, contrary to our expectations, the opposite has happened and the scientist is unaware, it is your art to guide the interviewer to your abilities and skills in the session and, in general, to manage the session.

For example, you may have skills, knowledge or strengths that the interviewer does not ask about, and it is your art to manage the discussion to mention your strengths.

Undoubtedly, one of your most important missions in an interview session is to show your passion and energy in addition to introducing your most important abilities. Therefore, one way to manage a meeting is to ask for permission and walk to a whiteboard or flip chart, if available, with complete confidence. List your skills and capabilities in a coherent and categorized way. You can even draw a horizontal axis from birth to the future and mark the most important years of your life, what you have done and what you have learned, and so on. Write your future plan for the coming years.

In my opinion, such an action miraculously conveys a positive and incredible feeling to the interviewer.

7. Never lie

I am not going to talk about the ethics and condemnation of lying in this book, but I must point out that dishonesty can completely ruin the outcome of an interview. It is enough for the interviewer to realize that honesty has not been observed in answering the questions. Experienced interviewers for sure validate some of the answers. For example, if he asks, "What was the last book you read?" The next question may be for you to explain what the book is about. If the job seeker uses professional terms, the interviewer may ask him/her to explain more about the word. In addition, interviewers make a judgment about honesty, depending on the job applicant's response, and if he says something wrong, he will become confused and the interview session gets more challenging for the applicant.

Of course, nothing is better than honesty, and if you do not know something or have nothing to offer, say it honestly. This honest confession of ignorance will have a positive effect on the interviewer's mind and sometimes is considered a positive point.

8. The issue of money is the last topic of discussion

It's the art of the applicant to achieve the highest payment for a job in an organization. This is not something that happens in an interview. In fact, this goal should be achieved by continuing to work and increasing knowledge and skills. Accordingly, from my point of view, salary issues should not be included in the initial talks at any cost. If your interview is to take place at several levels or in several sessions, delay the discussion of salary as much as you can, as this can lead the interviewer to a point of judgment where his or her opinion changes about you or even stops the discussion process. What's more, the more you show your abilities, the better your chances of getting paid when you get a job.

Likewise, if the interviewer asks you about salary and there are still other open discussions, respectfully ask him or her to postpone dealing with salary. For example, consider these sentences:

- I think there are much more important issues that we have not addressed yet.

- I believe it is too early to talk about it. For the time being, we must try to identify what we have in common.
- I do not deny that the salary discussion is one that I look forward to, but it is less important than other issues we haven't discussed yet.
- In a joking tone: Am I going to get paid by you!?
- If we make other cooperative issues clear, the issue of salary can be postponed to the end.

Obviously, we have to talk about salary in the end. If you can accept a slight fluctuation in income and are confident about your work output, it is a good idea to offer to work in the new job for a few months and then sit down to discuss salary issues. Otherwise, if it is decided to talk about payment in the interview, do not forget that talking about payment in the previous workplace is the weakest argument. Instead, you can talk about the basics of life. In this case, the interviewer is less likely to react. These sentences may be useful for salary discussions:

- I have to determine my salary in line with the quality of my work. Therefore, I cannot announce my requested salary. But in general, I have arranged my life in such a way that if I do not earn at least X per month, I will have problem meeting my needs.
- My minimum living expenses are X. If I have a lower income, I will not be able to cover these.
- I am ready to start working with at least X, which is the minimum need of my life, and after a few months, we will discuss salary together and look at the quality of my work, decide on the amount of salary, and if you are satisfied with my work quality, you can pay the difference for the first few months.
- I believe in the quality of my work so much that I know the organization will raise my payment, so I am content with

X, which is my minimum living expenses.

In any case, never conclude the salary amount and avoid using statements that hinder negotiation.

9. Put yourself in the place of the interviewer

In the previous pages, we talked about meeting management. One way that can help you better manage your interview session is to put yourself in the interviewer's shoes and what they are looking for when asking a question.

I have to say that in many job interviews, the responses are so irrelevant that I sometimes doubt that the job applicant has heard my question! Therefore, my basic advice for the job seeker is to put himself/herself in the interviewer's position and know what information he/she wants to get.[12] For example, when an interviewer asks about your abilities, he or she is asking if you have a specific

---

[12] I repeat that the job applicant is not going to say anything untrue. But we need to know what information the interviewer wants to get.

expertise or output that would work for the organization.

Therefore, it is better to address these points or if he asks about your limits for working hours, he wants to hear that you have no limits to work outside the official working time.

In my view, by all the questions the interviewer raises, he or she seeks to discover the "passion" of the job seeker above all. If you can show your desire and thirst to work in the organization during the interview and questions, you will definitely win the interview. Moreover, all those who show their enthusiasm at work will be so rewarded for their work that they realize they must always continue to work enthusiastically[13].

10. Take body language and tone of speech seriously

The body language of the job seeker is one of the

---

[13] The late American writer, Kurt Venhogut, has a unique saying: "We are what we pretend to be. So be careful what we pretend to be."

most important issues that is inadvertently affective even if the interviewer is not aware of it.

In the discussion of attire, reference was made to research conducted by several thousand interviewers. According to the same study and, of course, other similar studies, one-third of the interviewers said that in just ninety seconds, they would conclude whether the job seeker should be recruited or not.

In communication science, it is a well-known conclusion that the "first impression" by the other party is influenced by the following:

- 55 percent—the clothes, behaviour, and manners you enter through the door with
- 38 percent—tone quality, grammar, and confidence
- 7 percent—the words you use

All these show the extent to which nonverbal communication is effective and should be considered by the job seeker. According to research, the following nonverbal errors occur by job applicants in interview sessions:

- 67 percent do not make good eye contact.
- 38 percent do not smile.
- 33 percent do not have good posture.
- 33 percent are anxious.
- 26 percent shake hand weakly and inappropriately.
- 21 percent play with their hair or face.
- 21 percent sit with crossed hands on chest.

Accordingly, it is very important that the job seeker pays attention to the above points and is careful about the impact of their body language. A list of simple advice I can give to readers is as follows:

- If you have the choice of sitting on a chair or sofa, the chair is preferable as it is higher and you will not sink into it; you will sit at the same level as the interviewer.
- Another feature of sitting in a chair is that, basically, a table will be in front of you and you can hide your probable

anxiety behind the table. If you are not anxious, keep your hands under the desk as much as possible, except when you need to write something.

o Your smile will undoubtedly have a tremendous impact on the interviewer's mind and can even be seen as a symbol of energy and passion. Accordingly, smile recklessly.

o Be careful not to cross your hands over your chest unintentionally. This body posture will convey a sense of defence and negativity to the other person.

10. Be aware of common mistakes

There are a number of mistakes that applicants sometimes make and they should make every effort to avoid them. First of all, not paying attention to all the tips I have mentioned thus far is one of these mistakes. However, there are other things that, because they happen in interview sessions, I would like to mention:

- We may lose track of the main point of the interview and the interviewer follows us as well. The result of this mistake is the regret that will come to us after the interview—I wish I had talked about this or that issue. Again, this shows how crucial meeting management can be.
- We may get excited or angry during conversations. If we fall into this trap, the chances of being rejected in an interview are greatly increased. The interviewer may also use this technique to test the job applicant to ensure that the applicant can manage his or her behaviour and speech in the future if he or she is challenged by a client or co-worker.
- Depending on the current issues of the country, we may inadvertently enter into political issues. The interviewer may even deliberately do this to find out more about us. In such cases, the job seeker must ultimately withdraw

from the topic impartially and cautiously[14].

o The interview session may lead to religious, ethnic, racial, gender, etc. discussions. It is a big mistake for the applicant to get into any of these cases and he should avoid it by all means.

The applicant may be involved in insignificant issues in the interview. This is also a mistake that can change the opinion of the interviewer (especially for someone who is applying for a job at a higher position of the organization). For example, whether or not the company has a shuttle service, whether it offers lunch or not, whether it is closed on Thursdays or not, should not be an issue for the applicant to address in the interview.

12. You also ask your questions

---

[14] For example, the interviewer may say, "A faction voted in the election yesterday." The applicant can very diplomatically neutralize the discussion by saying, "I hope everyone who will be elected will take actions that meets the interests of the whole country and all Iranians. Principally, national speeches are the most impartial speeches that do not harm anyone."

Once you are sure that everything has been asked by the interviewer and there is no need to drag the discussion to the forgotten topics, it is now your turn to ask questions.

Before asking a question, keep in mind that addressing trivial issues will have a negative impact on the interviewer's mind. On the other hand, by asking important points, not only can you gain useful information for the future but you can also convey a positive feeling to the interviewer. These are simple examples of such questions:

- When can I get a job description for this organizational position?
- What are the most important challenges of this job?
- What exactly do you expect from the owner of this position?
- Why were previous employees in this role unable to satisfy the organization?
- In the coming months, what do I need to achieve to be successful in your point of view?

- Will I be cooperated to hear the expectations of different managers of the person in this position?
- If I am hired, can I ask you to let me present my plan and review its progress periodically?

***

What has been said so far is concise and hasty material to increase the likelihood of being hired in an organization, which of course, could have been far more extensive, but from what I believe, the length of discussions and the thickness of the book will prevent it being read thoroughly. Hence, I will suffice to say this briefly. However, in my opinion, if the job seeker follows the tips in this book, he or she will most likely be able to get a job in the organization of his or her choice.

Chapter Five:
Post-employment tips

Everything that has been explained so far was for the job seeker to be able to enter the organization. These are just some of the goal setting initial efforts that you can try to enter the organization which is in accordance with your individual development plan. In fact, it is after being hired that we have to make a real effort and achieve the desired goals.

One of the dangers that threatens us all after employment is the death of longing and getting used to our possessions. In fact, sometimes we quickly forget how much we longed to be hired in the organization, and this may cause us to give up trying to grow and prosper in our role.

Sometimes I give this example to my young friends that trying to grow in the organization is like the wings flutter of birds while flying. If they stop fluttering at any time, we will see the bird descent and fall. One should not give up while working in an organization, otherwise, he/she will be pushed to the limit and sooner or later, he/she will have to leave the organization.

I considers the key to success at work to be the three elements of "honesty," "patience," and "effort," and I believe that if employees follow these three, their success at work is guaranteed. In the worst case, if the work environment of the organization is incredibly unsuitable, you can leave the organization, but in any case, it will be on the path of your own growth and in other organizations.

With this introduction, I would like to quickly make some tips as "tips for success and growth" in organizations. However, I know it very well that elaborating these points requires a better opportunity and I will suffice mentioning a few general points.

1. Preparing a personal development plan at work and life

The necessity and importance of a personal development plan was sufficiently discussed in this book. However, I need to remind you that if you did not have such a plan by the time you were hired by an organization, spend time and prepare it. The first step in preparing a personal plan is to have a realistic image of yourself.

Hold a pen and write down your future destination for years to come. I even recommend that you share the plan with your manager to let them know that you have a specific plan in mind of where you want to go. From my point of view, for a manager there is nothing sweeter to know than the fact that subordinate is working with a specific passion and plan.

It may even be a good idea to schedule seasonal or annual meetings with your manager to consult with him or her and analyse how much you have grown in your personal life and hear his or her suggestions for improvement.

2. Put honesty and transparency first

Transparency and honesty are some of the desirable traits that can help people grow in organizations where their basis is business affairs. Expediency and lack of transparency are the enemy of your long-term growth and success. What to say to please others, to show the truth in a different way, etc., are all things that make us unqualified personnel, and if we use the best methods in pretending, sooner or later, an unscrupulous human image of us will be presented to the organization and others.

It is your art to behave in such a way that makes you a symbol of honesty in the organization, because the organization will rely on you in a situation where it has full confidence in your honesty. While honesty and transparency will be effective in managing your communications in the organization.

3. Proper management of social relations with people in the workplace

One of the biggest weaknesses of workforces that

do not grow properly in organizations is that of social relations. In all the studies that have been done on the key skills of people in organizations, it has been concluded that communication management is the most important skill of people, regardless of their organizational level.

In this regard, there are so many remarks and advice that it can be said without exaggeration that a person learns about it as long as he is alive. That is why it is recommended that communication skills with others must be considered as the most important pillar of progress in the organization on the agenda of the reader, because our biggest common point with each other is that we "rarely" feel weak in this regard.

4. Sharing your knowledge and experiences with others

There is a misconception among some of us that if we share our knowledge and experience, others will become a danger to us or take our place. Ironically, successful people are those who generously try to help others grow and continue the path of learning and growth as well.

If you are looking to grow in the organization, create an image of yourself that you are always looking to educate and grow others by your actions. As in the management literature today, it is said that a leader is not someone who trains good followers, but someone who trains good leaders[15]. All in all, by taking such an approach, you will always be looking to grow and learn.

5. Expressing enthusiasm and moving towards challenges and accepting new responsibilities

If you want to grow faster in the organization, you must always be thirsty for new responsibilities. By accepting new responsibilities and taking on challenges, you can force yourself to learn better and grow in the organization. So, if a situation arises in which you can take on a new job or task, take the initiative and accept it or suggest that you accept it no matter how much it pays you, be in charge of doing it.

---

[15] "The function of leadership is to produce more leaders, not more followers." - Ralph Nader

In fact, by doing so, you will discover the hidden potential of your learning and grow in the organization, and you will experience the sweetness of achieving results.

I have learned over the years that for personal growth, I cannot hope for the day when I have enough time and opportunity to start a new business or activity. That is why most of the time I expose myself to doing something. For example, I take on a new responsibility or I set out to speak on a topic at a conference. Accepting this new responsibility means staying up late and cursing myself in the future. But after doing so, I learn a lot of new things and the joy of achieving the result is indescribable.

6. No boundaries for responsibilities

One of our mistakes in the organization is to think that we are working in a certain unit and that other matters of the organization have nothing to do with us.
If you want to grow fast in the organization, never forget that everything in the organization relates to

us. Therefore, if, for example, we work in the technical department, but the sales department does not have a suitable website, it is definitely our responsibility to remark our recommendations and reflect them to the relevant managers in the organization. Or, if the organization's elevator is not clean, it is also relevant to me as an accounting employee and I must pursue the problem compassionately until the problem is resolved.

If the organization in which you work has a system of suggestions, make sure to spend time and energy on various issues of the organization and always ensure that the best suggestions are made by you.

Sometimes I hear some young friends say, "What good is it for me to spend time doing something that has nothing to do with me?" While the enemy of growth and success in the organization is that you calculate everything and want to immediately consider what you receive for each action you take. In fact, in such a situation, you should seek your benefit in the long or medium term.

7. Accepting your responsibilities and mistakes

Some of us are less accustomed to admitting our mistakes and try to compensate for them. We often hear the phrase, "The word of the man is one," while only the word of the ignorant man is the same, because we are experiencing and learning in life and work. Even if we make a mistake, every time we find out about something, we can boldly admit our mistake.

It is important that our actions and activities in the organization are with good intention. In this case, if we have made a mistake unintentionally, we can accept the mistake and take responsibility for it and apologize.

Contrary to popular belief, an apology can be a symbol of the strength and stability of the workforce in the organization. Everyone can make mistakes; the important thing is to learn from it and try not to repeat it again.

One of the obvious idiocies in an organization when an error or mistake occurs is that it seeks to keep the issue secret or to justify the mistake or to project blame on others. Rather, the ideal is that in such a case, we do not let the subject become obsolete or hope to remain hidden. However, we have to confess wrongdoings, apologize, and try to make up for them.

8. Confession of ignorance and request for training

As in the previous case, if there are cases at work that you do not know about, there is nothing wrong with telling the person concerned or your manager that you do not have enough information about this and need training. The biggest mistake is to pretend to know things. In this situation, we have gambled on our image and reputation in the organization, and sooner or later, our honesty will be questioned.

If you do not have the required knowledge of work related to you in the organization, ask for help very clearly or ask to be trained. In the worst case that the organization refuses to do the training, you can ask for the opportunity to learn it yourself.

It is fascinating for your manager to see that you are eager to address your educational shortcomings, and if the manager is knowledgeable and forward-thinking, he/she will take the initiative to train you or assign people to share the knowledge you need.

9. Do outstanding work

As the advice presented in the interview section, one of the most important secrets of your success in the organization is to be different from others, and obviously the best way to do this is to do outstanding work in the organization. To do this, things must go beyond what your organization and manager expect. In other words, the quality of the work you do must be unique and different. In simple words, your unwritten signature should be felt at the bottom of the activity you are doing. For this purpose, you should try to get the highest quality and provide the deepest outputs in the organization. This cannot be achieved except by trying to gain knowledge and experience and continuous practice.

Unfortunately, there is a big problem in organizations where some employees have a simplistic and superficial view of things, and this prevents their work output from being prominent and distinctive. The first step to eliminating this complication is to practice looking at the issues and quality of work with a deeper perspective.

10. Provide solutions to the issues and challenges of the organization

Sometimes the staff look at top-level managers as problem solvers, and with the slightest problem, they ask their manager or supervisor what to do. Having such an approach makes us a passive force that neither intends to grow nor is willing to take responsibility.

We have to get used to the fact that whenever we want to ask our manager a question to make a decision, we have to prepare our answer or suggested solution in advance. Similarly, there are many people in the organization who are just protesting and complaining about issues but have no solution or suggestion to resolve them.

Therefore, if you ask your manager a question, be sure to state your suggested solution and ask him or her to make the final decision. With such action, you can develop and both demonstrate a problem-solving manner, which sends the message that you can deal difficult issues ahead. In addition, you will create a much better image of yourself in the minds of colleagues and managers.

11. Have a continuous study of content related to the activity

I reckon there is no need to emphasize the need for study. I know friends who have not yet bothered to read the basic documentation and the website of the organization in which he/she works!

This is the basic premise of all employees in the organization. In addition, successful employees need to keep themselves refreshed and informed by studying the areas of organizational activity in which they work. Fortunately, this can be done simply by accessing resources on the Internet.

It will be great if you are looking to study the latest developments in areas related to the organization, even if you are not the front line of units in which you work for.

By doing this, you will get a better or more complete picture of the current situation and the future of your organization. In addition, having knowledge beyond what is available in the organization can be one of your strategies to stand out from the crowd.

12. Communicate with people who are more successful than you

In the organization, the behaviour of successful people is very similar to each other, and similarly, unsuccessful people have incredible similarities. This is so common that, based on experience and hearing a few words from people, it is possible to understand in which category they fall.

Therefore, the basic advice is to identify successful and dynamic people in your newly hired organization and connect with them in any way that is appropriate.

By doing this, you can largely learn the approaches and attitudes of successful people at work and grow in the organization. At the same time, as mentioned in the previous lines, new responsibilities and challenges must be welcomed, and among the successful of the organization, such cases can be found better.

***

I admit that I have made this section on post-employment recommendations short—the recommendations are not limited to these topics—but addressing them is beyond the scope of this book.

Therefore, I suffice to express the wish that the contents of this chapter have been intriguing to the readers and that they will get prosperous results by applying the recommendations as soon as possible.

—Ahmadreza Nakhjavani

—F×M—

© Firouz Media 2022

www.ingramcontent.com/pod-product-compliance
Lightning Source LLC
Chambersburg PA
CBHW030309100526
44590CB00012B/575